The FIRST BOOK of
BEES

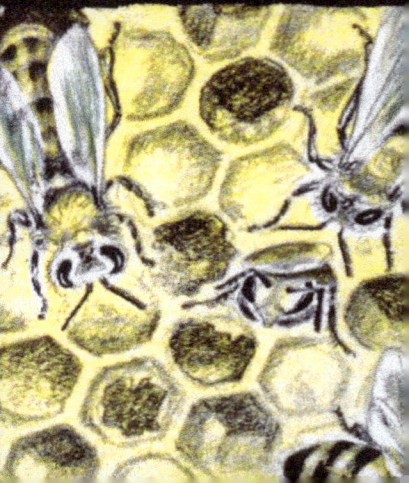

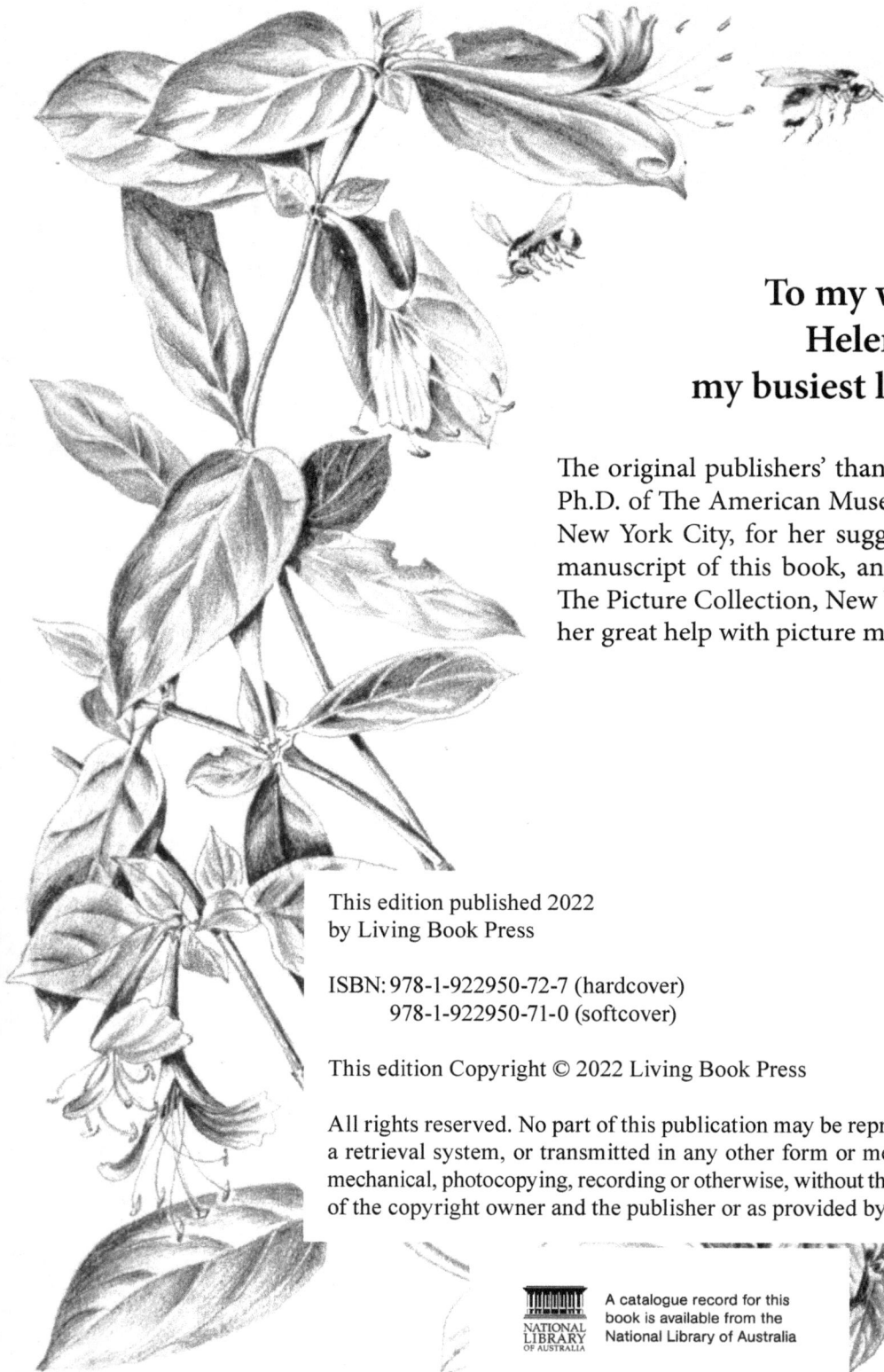

**To my wife
Helen
my busiest little bee**

The original publishers' thanks to Lucy W. Clausen, Ph.D. of The American Museum of Natural History, New York City, for her suggestions concerning the manuscript of this book, and to Ramona Javitz, of The Picture Collection, New York Public Library, for her great help with picture material.

This edition published 2022
by Living Book Press

ISBN: 978-1-922950-72-7 (hardcover)
978-1-922950-71-0 (softcover)

This edition Copyright © 2022 Living Book Press

NATIONAL LIBRARY OF AUSTRALIA

A catalogue record for this book is available from the National Library of Australia

The FIRST BOOK of BEES

By ALBERT B. TIBBETS

Pictures by
HELENE CARTER

BEES ARE ALWAYS WORKING

Almost any day in summer, you can find a bee buzzing around in a garden or field or orchard. If you stand still and don't strike at it, you will be able to look carefully and see what kind of bee it is. As a rule, bees only sting people who seem to be bothering them or interrupting their work.

For bees are always working. Some kinds of bees work alone and live by themselves. Scientists call them "solitary" bees. Other kinds live in groups called "colonies," and they work together.

Many of the bees you are likely to see are honeybees, the kind that make the honey we eat. They live in colonies.

The honeybees you most often see are beekeepers' honeybees that live in special boxes called hives, which have been set out for them. But there are others that are wild honeybees, who live the year around in hollow trees or in old barns, or in any safe, dry hole they can find. The wild honeybee colonies in this country were started when bees that people owned flew away from their hives and built colonies in the woods.

Some honeybees are brown or black and some have yellow bodies. But no matter what they look like, honeybees all live together in the same way. They all raise their young bees alike. They all make the honey that tastes so good on bread or pancakes. They all make the wax that we often use in candles or to polish furniture.

Of course, bees don't work for people on purpose. They make honey because it is their own food. They make wax to use in building their colonies. We are lucky that they often make more honey and wax than they can use. They will have much more than they need if the beekeeper who owns them helps them in various ways. This book will tell not only about honeybees and their unusually interesting lives, but also about the things a beekeeper does to make their work easier.

EACH BEE HELPS

There are many jobs to be done in a honeybee colony: keeping the hive clean, laying eggs, taking care of the young, storing away food, and other chores. This work is divided between two different kinds of bees in each hive: the queen and the workers. The queen lays eggs. The workers do all the other tasks.

The drones are a third kind of bee in each hive. They are fat and lazy and do no work at all.

Once a bee has grown into a worker, a queen or a drone, it can never change. Each sort, even a lazy drone, is useful to a colony, which needs all three kinds in order to go on living. Later on in this book you will find out more about how each one helps.

Queen Bee

Drone

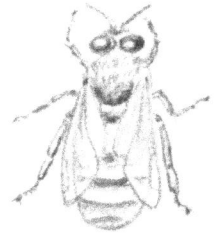

Worker Bee

MANY CHORES FOR WORKER BEES

But first, let's take a good look at a worker bee. It does very special work of many kinds. It collects nectar, a sweet liquid from flowers, and changes it into the honey that bees use for food. It gathers pollen, a fine powder found in flowers, and mixes it with nectar to make "bee bread," which is food for young bees. It helps build a storage place for all this food.

Worker bees are good housekeepers. They are nurses for the baby bees, too. There are always many jobs around a hive. Worker bees have lots to do, and they couldn't possibly get all their work done without special tools to help them. But the only tools they have to work with are the ones that grow right on their own bodies.

This is brood comb, where bee bread is stored as food to be used by newly hatched bee larvas.

BODIES WITH BUILT-IN TOOLS

A bee's body is divided into three parts. In front is the head. This has the eyes. Honeybees have good eyesight. They can recognize all colors but red, which they can't tell from black. And they seem to be able to recognize objects around their hives. They have a good sense of direction, so that they have no trouble in finding their own homes.

On their heads, bees also have two short feelers, which are noses, too. Bees have a keen sense of smell.

A worker bee's head has a mouth with strong jaws for chewing, and a long tongue with a spoonlike end. Around the tongue are parts somewhat like feelers. By using these and its tongue, a worker bee can make a tube to suck up nectar from flowers. A bee cannot cut the skins of fruit to suck the juices, but it can suck up juices from fruit already bruised and cut.

The middle part of a bee's body has four thin delicate wings, two on each side. A bee can move its wings very fast--as much as four hundred times a second—and worker bees can fly very far, sometimes eight miles in one flight.

Each honeybee has six legs—three pairs—on its middle part. Worker bees' legs have all sorts of little brushes and other tools to help them.

The hind part of a bee's body is the largest, and has several of the worker bee's important tools. There is a honey sac or "honey stomach," which is a sort of extra stomach where the bee stores the nectar it has sucked up with its tongue. Also in this hind section are some glands for making wax. This wax comes out of little slots on the under side of a bee.

On the back tip of a bee is a sting—a sharp point connected to poison glands. This is a bee's weapon for protecting its colony from enemies.

A worker bee uses its various tools to help it with its many, many jobs.

ARMED GUARDS

During the busy summer season, worker bees live for only about six weeks. They spend about the first three weeks of their lives as house bees, doing work inside the hives.

When a honeybee that is working in fields or gardens flies home to its hive, it lands on a kind of porch before its front door, which is a crack that runs across one side at the bottom of the hive.

At the door it has to pass guards. These are young bees that are really armed—they have their stings for weapons. They know by smell the bees that belong to their own hive, and they stand there at the entrance, ready to drive away any robber bees that may come from other colonies to steal honey. If the robbers don't fly off immediately, the guards sting them to death. The guards also watch out for mice and other invaders and sting them, too, if they try to sneak in.

House bees, cleaning cells

A bee lands on a kind of porch.

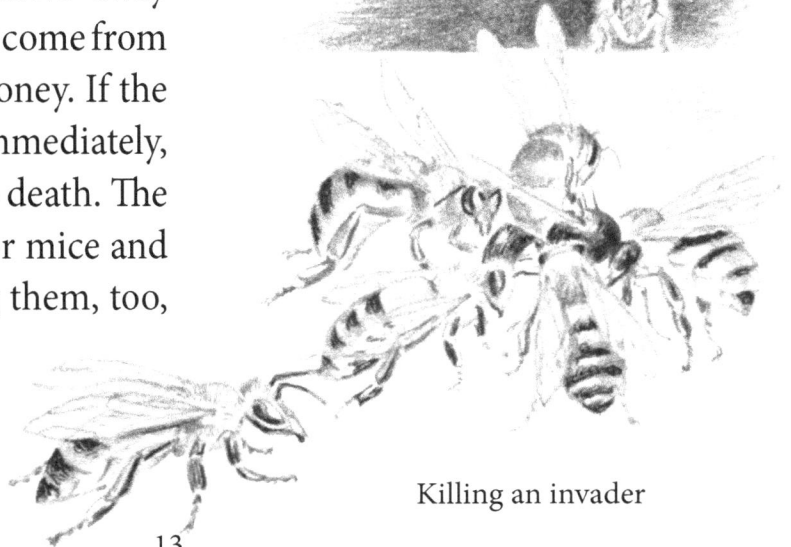

Killing an invader

13

Head of worker bee (enlarged)

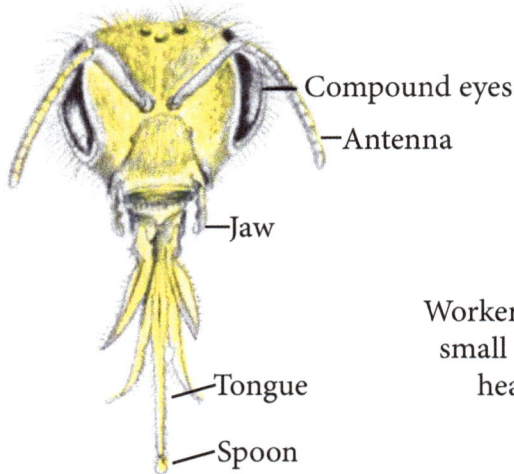

Compound eyes

Antenna

Jaw

Tongue

Spoon

Head of drone (enlarged)

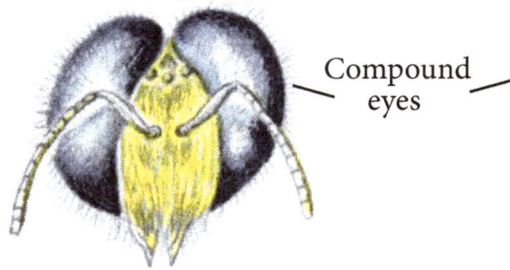

Compound eyes

Head of queen bee (enlarged)

Workers, drones and queens all have three small or simple eyes on the tops of their heads. These are also called ocelli.

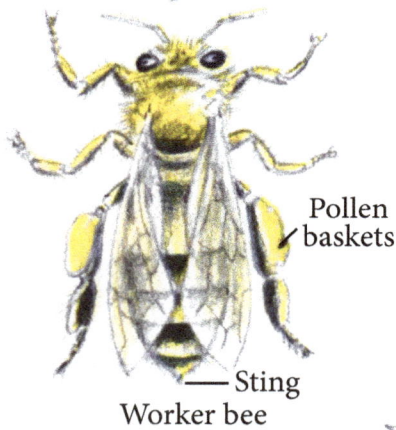

Pollen baskets

Sting

Worker bee

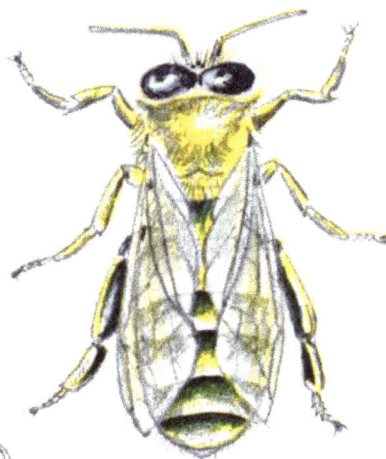

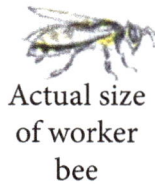

Actual size of worker bee

The drones are the male bees of a colony. They are large, noisy fellows, without any stings.

The queen is very important to a bee colony. She doesn't lead a life of leisure. She is kept busy, laying eggs.

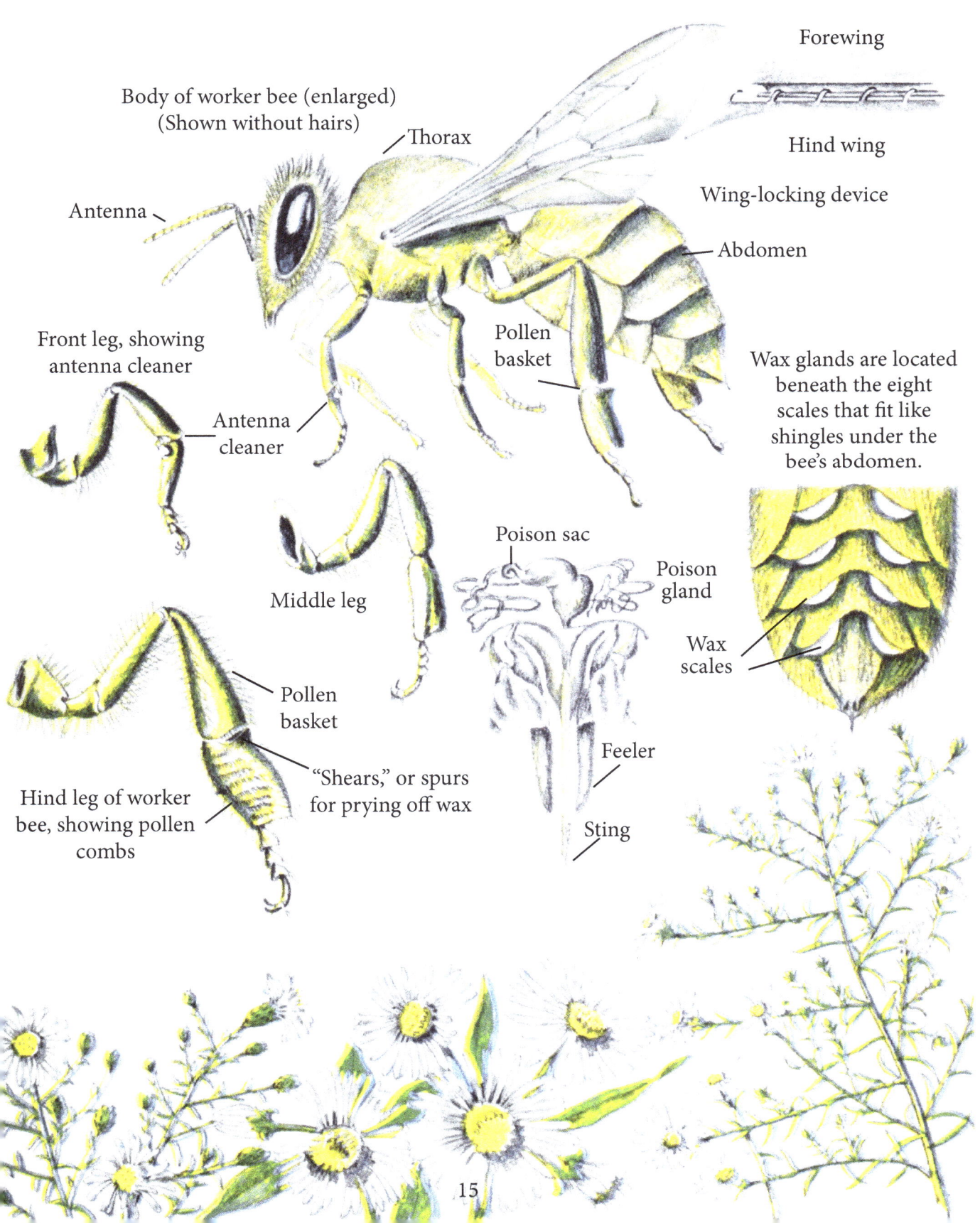

Body of worker bee (enlarged)
(Shown without hairs)

Thorax

Forewing

Antenna

Hind wing

Wing-locking device

Abdomen

Front leg, showing
antenna cleaner

Antenna
cleaner

Pollen
basket

Wax glands are located
beneath the eight
scales that fit like
shingles under the
bee's abdomen.

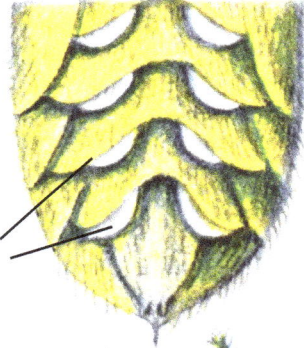

Middle leg

Poison sac

Poison
gland

Wax
scales

Pollen
basket

"Shears," or spurs
for prying off wax

Feeler

Hind leg of worker
bee, showing pollen
combs

Sting

AIR CONDITIONERS

Near the doorway of the hive are other bees that stand and make a humming sound, but not because they are angry. They make the noise with their wings, which they are fanning very fast, to do the work of air conditioners. Some stand on one side of the entrance, facing in, and some stand on the other side, facing out. Their fast-fanning wings keep the air circulating. The moving air cools the hive in hot weather and keeps the honey from getting too soft and runny. It also helps dry some of the moisture out of the new honey that the bees are making.

Taking a dead bee from the hive

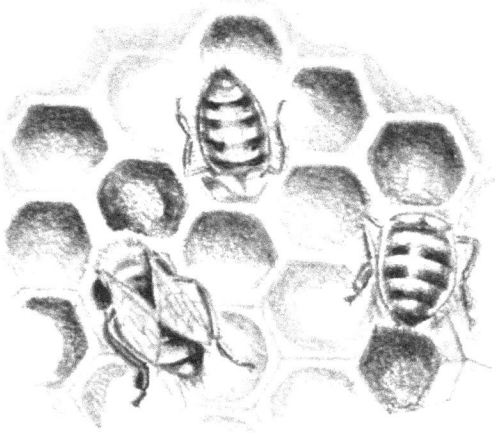

Worker bees, housecleaning

HOUSEKEEPERS

Other bees are at work cleaning up the hive. They crawl over the floor and carry out dirt or dead bees in their jaws. There isn't a great deal of dirt for them to clean up, because bees always take care of their toilet outside the hive.

When the guards have killed a mouse inside the hive, the cleaners have been known to seal it up in wax and propolis, a kind of glue from plants, to keep their home neat and free of smell.

A few bees do repair jobs around the hive. They use the propolis, which they gather from plants, to seal up any cracks in the outside walls where invaders might creep in or where the wind or rain could blow through.

Comb honey super

Food chamber

Brood chamber

Alighting board

BEES ARE BUILDERS, TOO

Some of the worker bees are building little six-sided wax cells in the hive. They are making what we call honeycomb, which is placed in two up-and-down layers, built back to back.

Bees use honeycomb for two different things. Some of the cells are cupboards for storing food. Others are little rooms for hatching and housing young bees until they are big enough to crawl around in the hive.

Inside their bodies, worker bees have special glands that change some of the honey they eat into wax for building honeycomb. A bee can change about six pounds of honey into one pound of wax.

When the liquid wax comes out of the eight little openings on the under side of a bee's body and reaches the air, it hardens. These bits of hardened wax on a bee's abdomen look like fish scales, except that they are much smaller, of course. They are flat and brittle, and if they were big enough you could see through them, almost as if they were glass.

Each worker removes her own wax scales by prying them loose with the spurs on one or the other of her hind legs. Then while she stands on her middle legs, she passes the scales to her front legs, and her front legs pass them to her mouth. Now she chews the wax until it is soft enough to be pushed or pulled into shape for building a cell.

When the wax is ready, the bee carries it in her jaws, or she may even tuck it under her chin, where she keeps it in place with her forefeet. She takes it to some cell that is being built. There another bee pinches off the wax with her jaws and pushes it into place on the cell wall.

A worker bee, removing wax scales

ALWAYS THE SAME SHAPE

Many bees work together on one cell, but the cells are always made exactly the same, in one or the other of two sizes, and they always have six sides. These sides fit together like pieces of a puzzle, so that there is no space wasted. Square cells would fit together just as closely, but honeybees' cells are never square.

Scientists have discovered that the six-sided cells are stronger than square cells would be.

This is a drone.

BORN SKILLFUL

Bees didn't figure that six-sided cells were best. Nor did they get together and think up all the other marvellous things they do. Bees—like other insects—can't think and plan ahead, the way human beings can. They don't really have knowledge. What seems like knowledge of how to make honey or six-sided cells is really "instinct"—a sense of how to do these things naturally, without ever being taught. Bees are born with all their skills. They don't have to learn the complicated jobs they do.

HONEYCOMB IN ROWS

Wild bees build all their own honeycomb, fitting it into the space where they live. But beekeepers have invented a way of making their bees build honeycomb in neat rows that can be lifted out and looked at now and then.

Beekeepers have square wooden frames that they put into the hives, placing about ten in a row, with space between each frame for the bees to move around in. The frames have a wide piece at the top, from which they hang, and the bees build their comb cells sideways across each frame, starting from sheets of wax called "foundations."

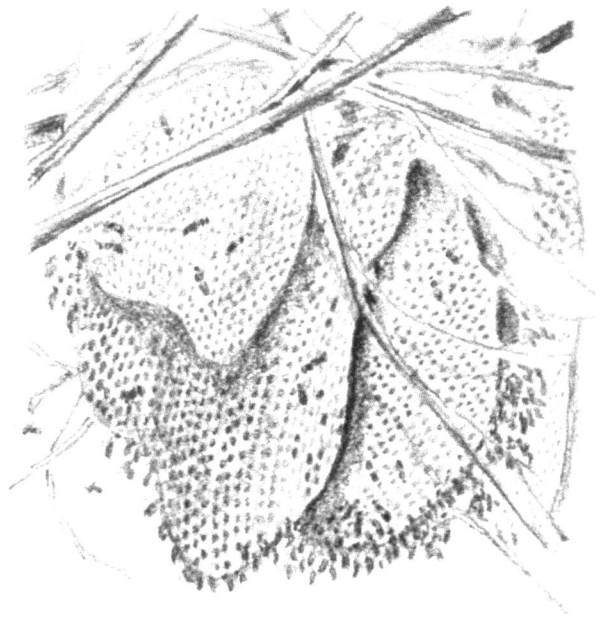

Inner wall of hive

Comb foundation

The bees will build this foundation out to a full comb.

SAVING TIME AND WORK

The reason for foundations is this: It takes a lot of honey and a lot of time for bees to make all the wax for their honeycomb, so beekeepers help them and give them a head start in building.

They buy flat sheets of beeswax that have been stamped so that they are covered with little six-sided ridges, to show the start of cells. These are the sheets called foundations, and they are like the foundations of buildings. The beekeeper fits them into the wooden frames that he puts in the hive, and the bees build comb from them.

When bees build comb from foundations, they look as if they were having a tug of war. One bee hangs onto a ridge in the wax. Another bee hangs onto the ridge next to it. Then one or more bees cling to each of these, and they all tug until the ridges have grown into walls on six sides. It is much quicker for bees to build this way from a foundation than to make the whole of each cell out of the wax that they grow in their bodies. So they have time to gather more nectar and make more honey.

HIVES THAT GROW TALLER

A beekeeper starts his hive with a ground floor, called a "brood chamber," and a second story. When the second story is nearly full of honey in frames, he takes off the top of his hive, adds a third story—another box full of frames—and the bees move into that. The beekeeper keeps building up his hive with more stories all summer long, as the bees make more and more honey and need more and more space for storing it. The second story of a hive is called the "food chamber" and that is where the bees keep most of the honey they use for their own food. The stories above the food chamber are called "supers."

Super

Super

Super

Super

Food chamber

Brood chamber

FINDING FLOWERS

All day long in warm sunny weather, some of the worker bees who are called "field bees" fly back and forth from the hive to the flowers where they suck up the sweet liquid called nectar. Sometimes they may travel four miles in their search for flowers.

Occasionally a bee who has returned to the hive from a food-hunting trip stands and sways her body from side to side. This is called a honey dance, and it tells the other bees that she has found a big supply. Very soon they will leave the hive to find the honey-nectar that made the dancing bee so excited.

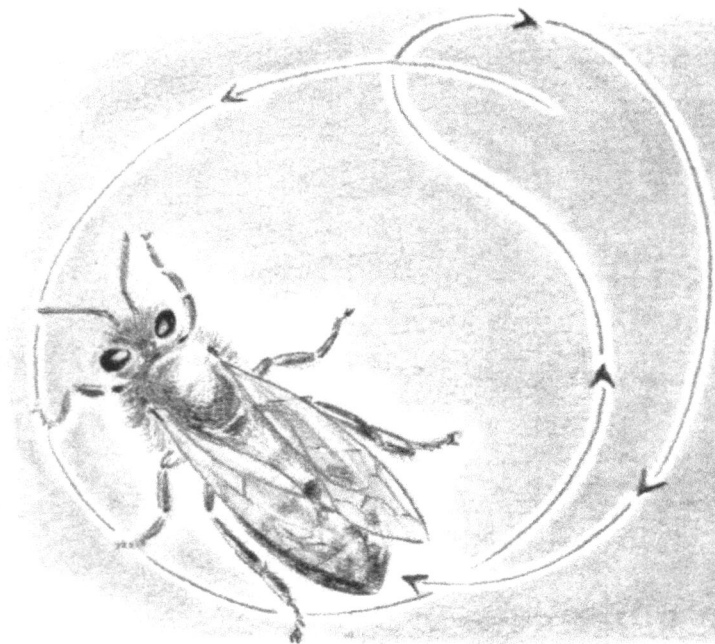

Round dance   Wagtail dance

In the round dance, the bee dances in circles. This dance seems to be performed when the source of nectar is near the hive.

In the wagtail dance, the bee dances a half circle to one side, then runs straight back to the starting point and dances a half circle to the other side. This dance seems to be used when the nectar is quite far away. Some scientists think it may indicate the distance of the nectar from the hive, so that the other bees can find it easily.

If you watch bees closely in a garden you will see that they work around certain flowers but pass others by. That is because the flowers are shaped differently. Some have their nectar where bees cannot get at it. Others, such as white clover and apple blossoms, are shaped so that a bee can sip the nectar easily.

Scientists have made experiments that prove a bee is guided to flowers by their color and scent. When she does her honey dance, the others probably smell the nectar she has found and brought back to the hive. They may use this scent as a clue to finding the same field or garden or orchard.

FLYING HOME

As soon as the field bee has sucked up nectar through her tonguetube, and it has gone into her honey sac, it begins to change. No one knows exactly what happens, but probably nectar is changed into honey by juices that come from glands inside the bee, just as saliva comes from glands in your mouth.

When a bee has filled her honey sac with as much nectar as she can carry, she flies back to the hive. Although she may have been wandering for miles from flower to flower, she always flies home in a straight line. That is why a straight line is often called a "bee line."

MAKING HONEY

Back at the hive, a field bee may give part of her load of nectar to a house bee. She opens her jaws and squeezes a drop of nectar out over her tongue. The house bee stretches her tongue out full-length and sips the nectar from the tongue of the field bee. Bees are most likely to do this on hot bright days when many flowers are in bloom and a great deal of nectar is flowing.

No matter which bee has the nectar, this is what happens next: The bee spends about twenty minutes squeezing the nectar in and out of her honey sac and rolling it around on her tongue. This takes some of the moisture out of the nectar. Probably some chemicals from the bee's glands are mixed with it, too, so that it is ready to ripen into honey.

STORING HONEY

Now the bee looks for a cell in the honeycomb where she can store her honey. She may find one in the comb that the workers have built on the ground floor of the hive. But she is more likely to take her honey to one of the upper stories.

When a bee with a load of honey finds a cell that is empty, she crawls in. Then she forces the honey out of her honey sac and uses her tongue as a brush to paint the honey onto the top of the cell walls. If she finds a cell in which there is already honey she just adds another drop to it.

So that a bee can crawl into a cell, her wings unhook where they were fastened together on each side for flying, and slide, one on top of the other, becoming very narrow. Without her hooking and unhooking apparatus, a bee could never crawl into a honeycomb cell to do her work.

MORE ABOUT HONEY

When the cell is full, the honey is still quite thin. More moisture has to be dried out of it to keep it from spoiling. This is the job of the air-conditioners, who stand at the hive entrance, fanning with their wings to keep a little breeze circulating. During the busiest time, when many flowers are blooming, bees are busy day and night. Field bees bring in the nectar as long as there is daylight, and house bees work even after dark, keeping the air moving through the hive.

After the honey in a cell is thick enough, workers cover it with wax. Sealed up in the comb, honey will keep for a long time. And the longer it keeps, the better it tastes.

Bees live on the honey they make. It is their food. But grown-up bees do not always wait for the honey to be fully ripened before they eat it. They sip the nectar or honey with their tongues, either from a cell or from the tongue of another bee. Usually a field bee takes a small meal this way before she starts on a trip to look for more nectar.

A BEE'S KIND OF BREAD

Besides nectar, bees also collect pollen and make it into another kind of food. Pollen comes from the flowers where the bees find nectar. It is a kind of dust inside the flowers which helps to grow seeds and fruit.

A bee's body is thickly covered with short little hairs. Some pollen rubs off onto the hairs accidentally as the bee crawls down into the heart of a flower looking for nectar. But she also scrapes pollen off on purpose with her jaws and mixes it with nectar in her mouth.

Then, while the bee is flying, all six of her legs go to work so fast you can hardly believe it. The front two gather pollen from her body with their brushes, and mix it with the moist pollen from her jaws. This moist ball of pollen is then taken by the pollen brushes on the middle legs. Then with the combs and brushes on her hind legs, the bee takes the pollen and packs it into her pollen baskets. Her right hind leg packs pollen into the left basket, and her left leg packs it into the right basket. In no time at all she has gathered two lumps of pollen that look much too big for her to carry.

The pollen and nectar a bee collects for one load weigh almost as much as she does herself. After she reaches the hive with this big load, she climbs around on the comb, looking for a cell in which to store it. When she finds an empty cell she grasps its upper edge with her front two legs. Her other four legs are inside the cell and her abdomen hangs outside. Now her middle pair of legs force the pollen out of the baskets on her hind legs.

The field bee who has collected the pollen then usually goes off and lets a house bee finish packing the pollen into the cell. House bees do not take pollen from field bees as they take nectar, but after the pollen is in a cell they crawl in head-first and mash it down. They also add honey and perhaps some juices from their mouths to preserve the pollen. Now they have what is called "bee bread." House bees seal the cell with wax and leave it until the bee bread is needed as food for baby bees. Grown bees never eat bee bread.

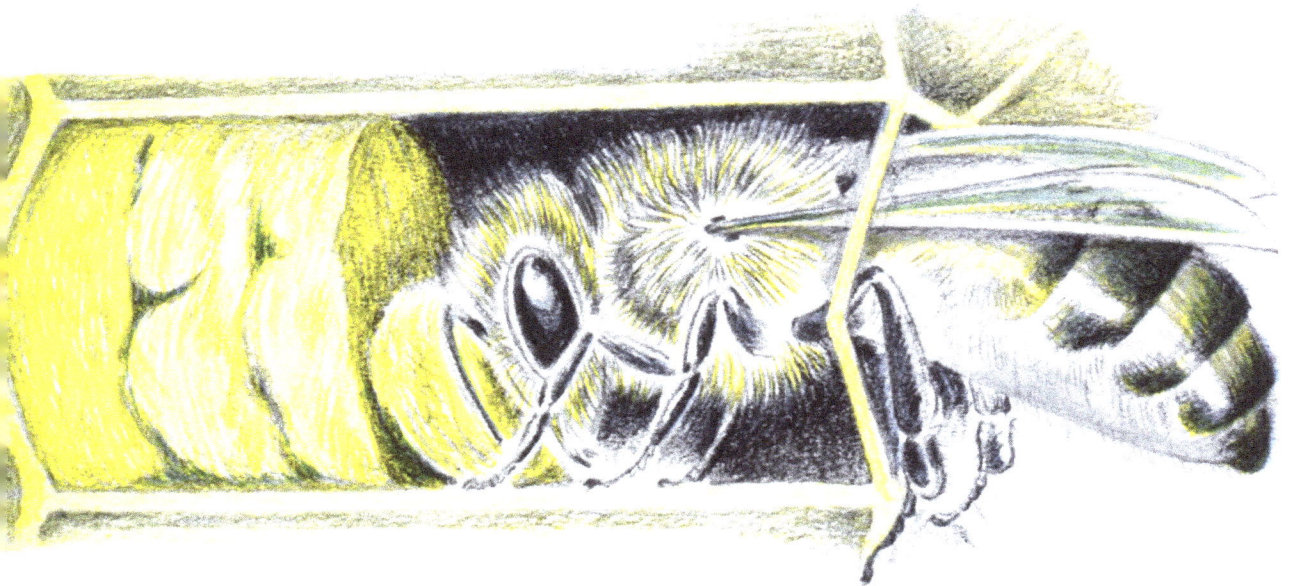

Cross section of a cell, showing bee bread being mashed down by a house bee

THE MOST IMPORTANT BEE

All of the bees who take care of the hive and bring in food are female bees, and they are all worker bees.

Besides them, one special female bee in every hive is the queen. Her body is beautiful and shiny, and she is much bigger and longer than the workers. She is the mother of all the bees, and she does all the egg-laying. That is her only job.

The queen is the most important bee in the hive. She sometimes lays as many as a million eggs altogether. A strong colony has between fifty and eighty thousand bees in it at honey-making time. So the queen has to lay a lot of eggs.

The workers are never too busy to take good care of her. A few of them always go around with her in the hive to feed her and keep her clean.

A drone, on the right, receiving food from a worker bee

BEES THAT DON'T WORK

In the midst of all the busyness of a beehive, the drones crawl around clumsily and don't do any work at all. They are the male bees. They can't gather nectar because their tongues aren't shaped right. They have no pollen baskets for gathering pollen. They are not fitted to do any of the work inside the hive. They do not even have stings, so they cannot work as guards. The drones are noisy, awkward fellows, always buzzing and tumbling about and getting in the way. Sometimes the worker bees even push them out of the hive to get rid of them.

The drones have only one purpose in the bee colony. When the old queen dies or stops laying enough eggs, a new queen takes her place. Before she starts her egg-laying, the new queen mates with one of the drones, who becomes the father of the new bees. So, although the drones take no part in the work of the hive, they really are necessary to the life of the whole colony.

This kind of hive is almost alway used in the United States today.

Hives like this, made from a rope of twisted straw, are still used in some parts of Europe today.

The small cups on the under side of this modern hive are filled with wheel grease. Ants, trying to steal honey, bog down in the grease.

Early settlers in America used straw beehives. Sometimes they built roofs over them, to protect them from sun and rain.

Rough wooden hives, or bee "gums"—sometimes made from the trunks of trees—are still used in some places in the southern United States.

QUEEN OF THE HIVE

When a new queen is ready to look for a mate she flies from the hive and finds a number of drones easily because of their loud buzzing. After making herself known to them, the queen starts flying up and up into the air. All the drones follow her, and the swiftest and strongest one finally catches her. They mate and the queen returns to the hive. In a few days she will begin to lay eggs.

Usually a queen mates only once in her lifetime, but she can often go on laying eggs for two or three years afterward. All during the time that nectar is flowing she lays eggs, with only brief rests. She stops if there is a spell of bad weather that keeps the workers from gathering nectar, but she starts again when they do. Then, when frost kills the flowers in the fall, she stops for the winter. In spring, she begins again when field bees start bringing in nectar.

As long as the queen lays eggs, the workers pay great attention to her. They stand around in a circle, ready to feed her. As she moves about in the hive she waves the feelers on her head. She can tell which workers have honey to give her by crossing her feelers with theirs. The workers open their mouths, and the queen puts in her tongue to suck up the honey. They clean her and caress her and comb her hair with the combs on their legs. They even bathe her with their tongues. All this attention seems to help her lay many eggs.

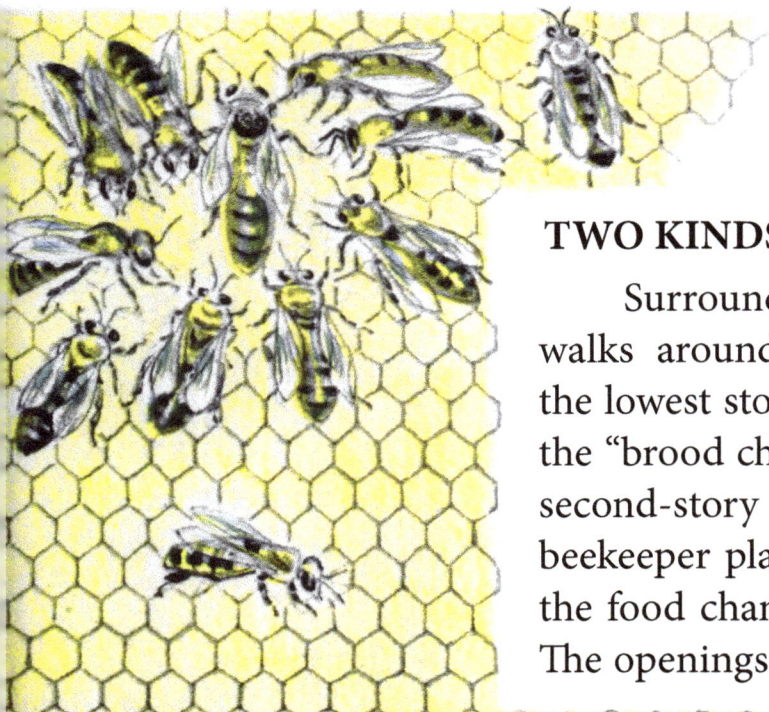

TWO KINDS OF EGGS

Surrounded by workers, the queen walks around over the comb, usually in the lowest story of the hive, which is called the "brood chamber," but sometimes in the second-story food chamber, too. Often a beekeeper places a sort of grating between the food chamber and the supers above it. The openings in the grating are big enough for the workers to go through, but not for the queen, who is larger than they. So she can lay her eggs only in the bottom two sections of the hive.

Remember that bees make the six-sided wax cells of the honeycomb exactly alike in two sizes. Most of the comb is made up of the smaller-sized cells. Bees use these for storing honey and bee bread. The queen also uses the

These cells are the exact size of cells used for storing honey and bee bread. The queen also uses them for laying her eggs. The cells for drone eggs are slightly larger.

cells—both the smaller and larger ones. She lays her eggs in them.

First she inspects an empty cell. If it hasn't been cleaned and polished by the workers, she passes it by. If it is clean, she deposits a tiny egg in it. The egg is long and thin, and always stands on end in the cell.

Three days after the queen has laid her eggs, tiny grubs will hatch.

The most remarkable thing about the honeybees' egg-laying is this: A good healthy queen seems to lay one kind of egg in the larger cells and another in the smaller cells. The eggs all look exactly alike, but they develop into two different kinds of bee. The ones in the smaller cells turn out to be workers. The ones in the larger cells turn out to be drones.

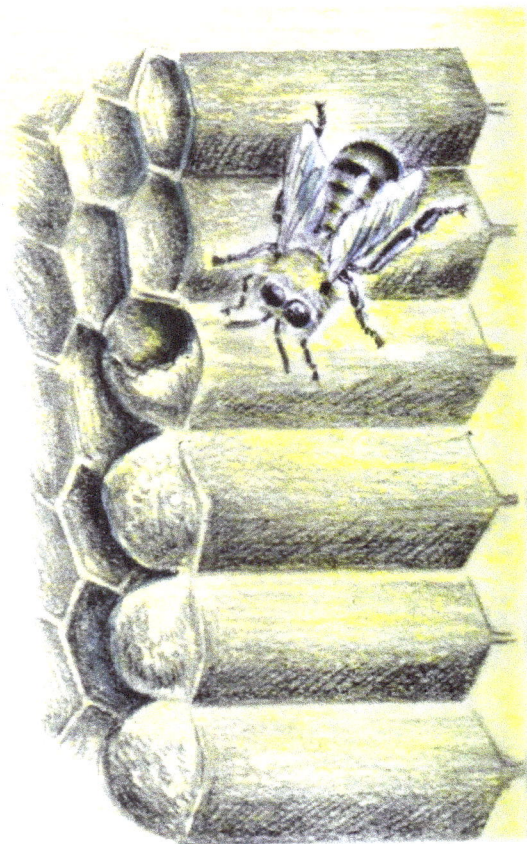

These are drone cells. They are larger than worker cells.

WHAT MAKES A QUEEN?

But if the queen lays only worker eggs and drone eggs, where do new queens come from?

They come from ordinary worker eggs—but they have been treated in a very special way.

From time to time, worker bees build over some of the small worker cells, making them larger until they are about the size and shape of small peanuts. They are now the largest cells in the hive. As the worker eggs in them hatch, nurses feed them differently from the just-hatched eggs in the small cells. From these ordinary worker eggs in the big peanut-shaped cells new queens will come.

Queen bees are made by worker bees!

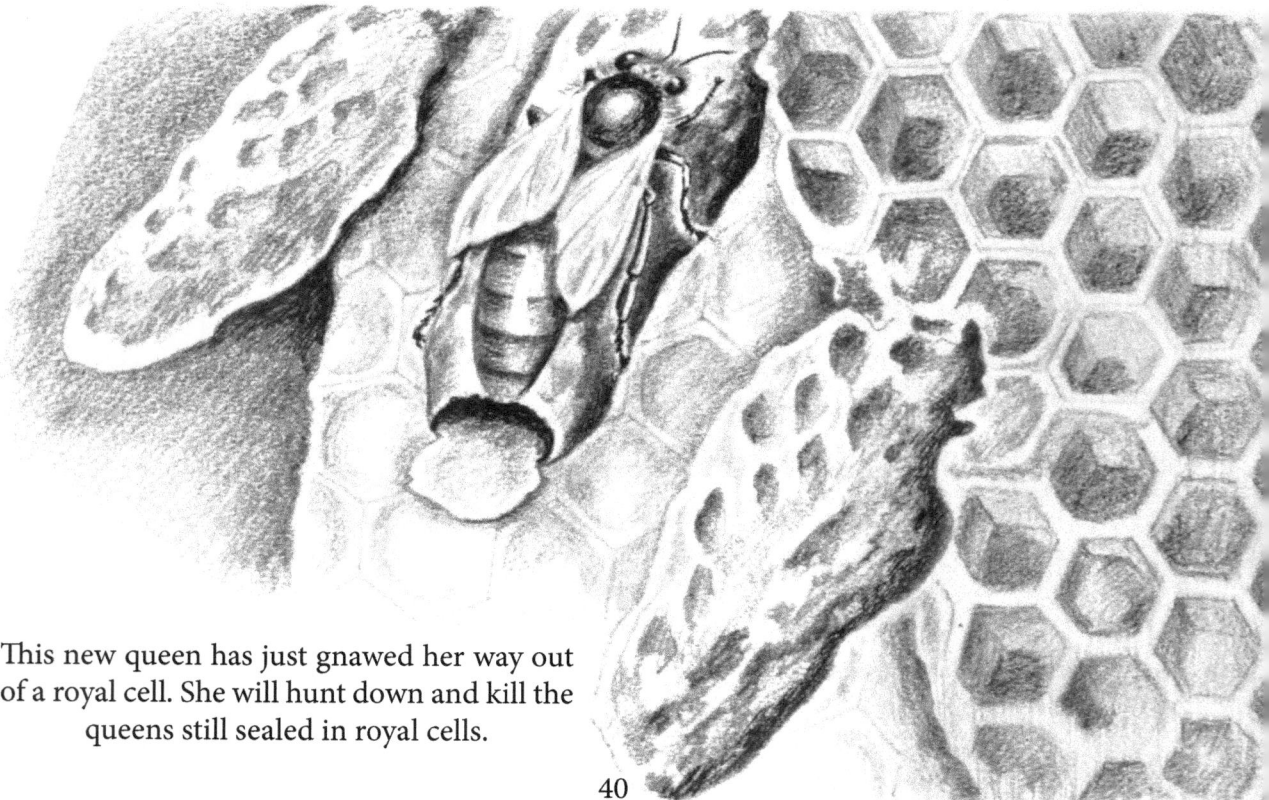

This new queen has just gnawed her way out of a royal cell. She will hunt down and kill the queens still sealed in royal cells.

40

BEGINNING TO GROW

Every bee—worker, drone, or queen—goes through four stages while it is growing up. After the queen lays an egg in the bottom of the cell, the nurse bees keep a close watch over it. Just before it hatches, in three days, a nurse bee puts into the cell a small amount of food called "royal jelly." No one is quite sure yet what royal jelly is, but most scientists believe that it comes from glands in the nurse bees' heads. The glands make the royal jelly out of foods and chemicals in the bees' bodies.

When the egg has hatched, the second stage in a bee's life begins. The bee is now like a little worm. It is called a larva.

The nurse bees keep on feeding the larvas. They run around

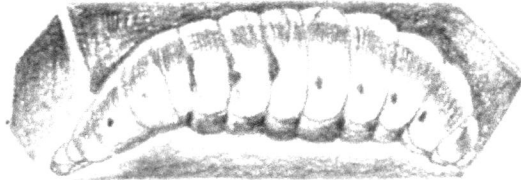

from cell to cell, making sure that each tiny worm is all right and that it has enough to eat. Often they don't leave it unwatched for more than two minutes.

For three days, all the larvas live on royal jelly. Then the nurse bees begin to feed most of them the nectar and pollen that has been made into bee bread and stored in cells nearby.

But the larvas in the built-up queen cells go right on being fed royal jelly, instead of bee bread. And this difference in feeding makes them into queens.

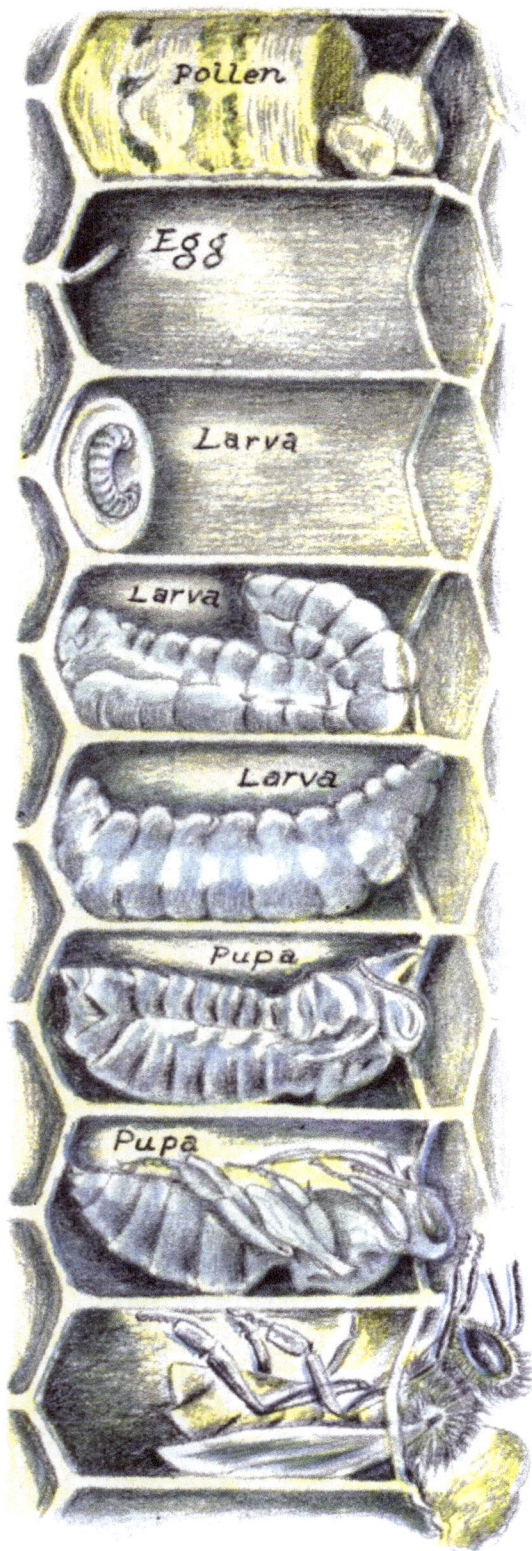

Pollen

Egg

Larva

Larva

Larva

Pupa

Pupa

Twenty-one days go by from the time a worker egg
is laid until a worker bee comes out of its cell.

SEALED IN

At first the larva is shaped like the letter C, but as it grows it straightens out, with its head toward the opening of the cell. As it gets bigger it sheds its skin several times. Then its cell is capped with wax by the workers, and the larva within makes itself a cocoon. The covering on the young bees' cells is slightly arched and is darker than the covering on honey cells. Drone cells are arched more than worker cells because drones are bigger. The queen cells are pulled out into their peculiar peanut shape.

FINALLY HATCHED

When the cocoons are safely sealed into cells, the young bees start their third stage: the "pupa" stage. Inside the cocoon a great change takes place. The wings and eyes and strong mouth parts begin to form and grow. The simple wormlike creature is becoming a complicated bee.

At last the bee is fully formed and ready to come from the cell. Now it gnaws its way through the wax and climbs out. It takes a queen sixteen days to grow, from the time she is laid as an egg until she comes out as a real bee. Workers take twenty-one days, and drones take twenty-five.

THE FIRST DAYS

Almost as soon as the young bee leaves the cell it commences to comb itself with the combs on its legs. Then it finds a food cell filled with honey and has a good meal. At first the young worker bees are fuzzy and feeble, but before long they are strong enough to clean and polish the cells in which the queen will lay eggs. Young worker bees also act as nurse bees; they make wax for new cells; and they help ripen the honey and pack it into the honeycomb. They are usually a week or ten days old before they take their first flight outdoors.

Some of these young worker bees have just crawled from their cells, others are still coming out.

A QUEEN'S LUCK

What happens with new queens is quite different. In the first place, they may not even get out of their cells at all, if the old queen is alive, because one queen almost never allows another in the hive. If she finds a big peanut-shaped cell, she opens it and kills the baby queen inside.

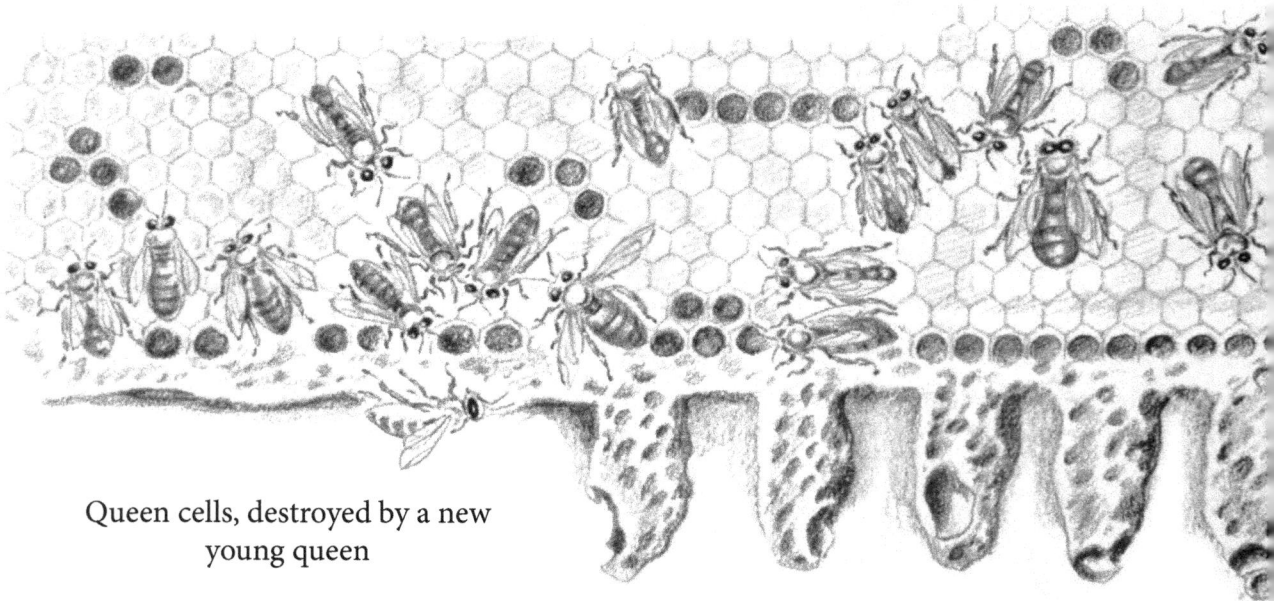

Queen cells, destroyed by a new
young queen

Sometimes the old queen doesn't see the queen cell before the bee is hatched. When that happens she tries to sting to death the new queen who has come out of a cell. Once in a while a young queen and an old queen have a real battle while worker bees stand around and watch without interfering. Whichever queen wins the fight by killing the other becomes the queen of the hive.

If a queen fails to be a good egg-layer, the workers get rid of her. They push her out of the hive, where she will starve because she can't gather nectar by herself. Or they may just seal her up in wax.

But when a bee colony has no queen it dies out very soon. In order to have new queens in case of some emergency, the workers build a few queen cells from time to time, even if the old queen seems to be doing a perfectly good job.

MOVING DAY

Sometimes bees get too crowded in a hive. Then a large number of them fill themselves up with honey and leave, all at once. This is called "swarming." Once in a while a colony swarms for no reason that the beekeeper can figure out. They just pick up and go.

Often, before they swarm, workers make extra queen cells, so that there will be a good chance of having a queen who will leave with them. An old queen doesn't always leave when the other bees go. Many beekeepers clip the wings of the queen after she has mated, so she can't fly even if she wants to. If no queen goes along when workers leave the hive, they return to it.

As the swarming bees rush from the hive, they circle around in the air, all together, and they often make as much noise as a small airplane. Sometimes the queen leads the swarm from the first. At other times she joins it after about half of the swarming bees have left the hive.

Gradually, as the bees circle around in the air, they draw closer and closer together. Finally they settle down on something like a tree branch, where they hang all together like a big bunch of bananas.

Bees who act as scouts then leave the cluster and go out looking for a new home. Sometimes the scoutbees even look for a new home before the swarming begins. But whenever they look, they have some way of getting the other bees to follow them to the place they have selected. It may be an empty hive or a space in a house wall, or a hollow tree.

ROBBERS!

If bees in a hive have had a good summer in which to gather nectar, they will have enough food to last them all winter. But sometimes, if the weather is bad, there may be few blossoms in summer. Then bees from one hive may start to steal honey from another hive that doesn't have enough guards at its entrance.

Beekeepers say that when bees once start to rob they never stop. Apparently they find that the easiest way to get honey. So if a beekeeper finds a robber hive he has to kill all the bees in it.

It is easy to tell robber bees from bees that really belong in a hive. They always fly down to the hive porch with their legs spread out, ready to fly away if the guards spot them. If they manage to get in and steal honey they take so much they can't fly away without climbing up the side of the hive and jumping off into the air. They are so heavy they are like airplanes that need to get up speed before they can take off.

Saint Ambrose is the patron saint of beekeepers. Hives, called skeps, in his image can be seen in parts of Holland.

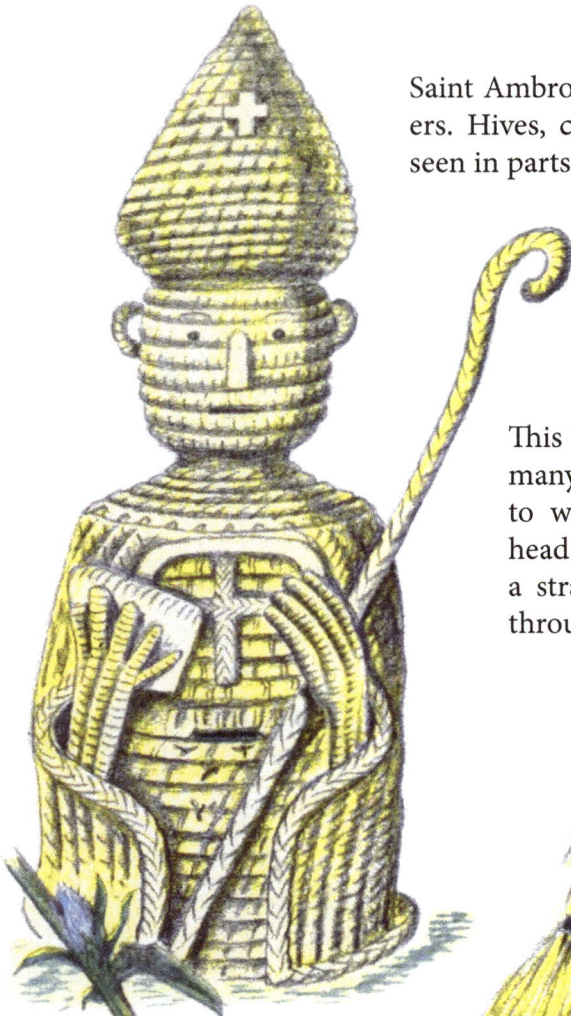

This hive from Hanover, Germany, was probably designed to ward off evil spirits. The head is made of crockery, on a straw skep. The bees enter through the mouth.

This rough covering protects the hive from rain and sun. Old-fashioned hives such as this are being replaced by modern ones.

50

In Turkey, the beekeeper stacks his box hives. The stonewall protects them from the wind, and the reed matting keeps out the cold and rain.

In some parts of Europe, wooden hives are carved in the likenesses of saints. The figures are from four to six feet high. In each one, a board in the front can be taken out. The bees go in and out through a small hole.

HOW BEES STING

Guards at the hives try to sting any kind of robber or invader—even people. Bees are more likely to sting when the weather is cold than when it is hot. They are cross and likely to sting shortly after a rain or when there has been very little nectar to make honey.

If you look at a worker bee's sting under a microscope, you will see two barbed spears connected with a red, eggshaped bag. This bag holds the poison which makes a sting swell up. Each of

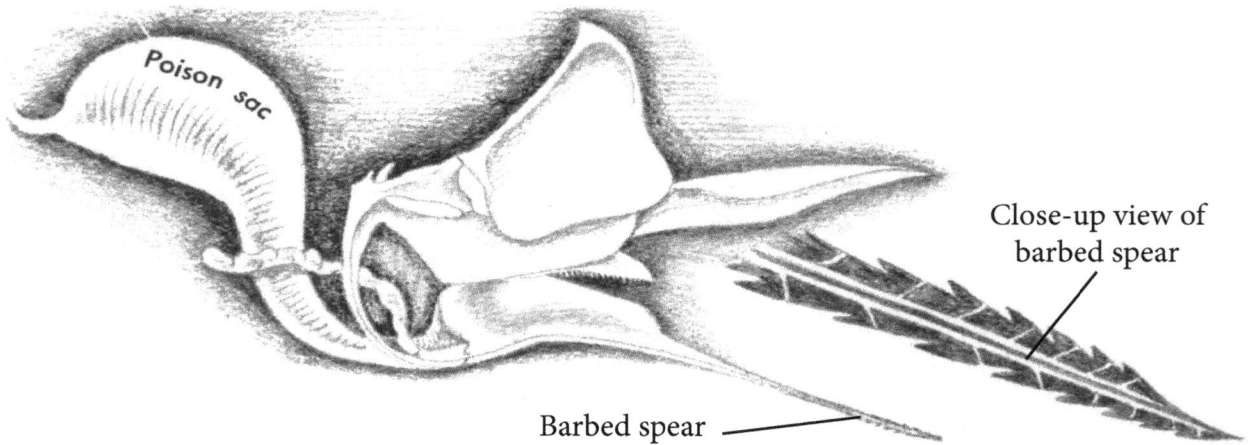

Poison sac

Close-up view of barbed spear

Barbed spear

the spears has several barbs like little fishhooks. The bee sticks one spear into an enemy until the barbs catch. Then she pushes the other spear until it also catches hold. After that she pushes first one spear in farther, then the other. As the barbs push in, poison from the little red sac runs down between the spears and starts to irritate the flesh.

Sometimes the barbs are so hard to pull out of the enemy's flesh that the bee has to leave them and the poison bag there in order to get away. When she does this, she dies.

Worker bees can usually get their stings out of other bees. They sting into the soft flesh between the joints in the bees' hard outer shells. Queens can sting other queens in this way and still live. Their stings are smooth, not barbed like the workers' stingers.

Usually worker bees cannot pull their barbs and poison bags out of people's skin, so they fly away without them. When this happens the bees die.

However, if you are stung, you aren't much interested in what will happen to the bee. You want to get rid of the sting as quickly as possible because it is painful. The best way is to *scrape* the sting off with a knife blade. If you pull it out with your fingers, the poison bag is squeezed and forces more poison into the little cut the sting has made. It is the poison that causes the swelling and pain.

There is nothing much to do when a bee has stung you. You may try putting hot wet cloths and then cold ones on the swollen place. This may help ease the pain somewhat. The best thing is to stay out of the bees' way unless you know how to handle them.

Bee, collecting propolis

AS WINTER COMES

As winter approaches, workers in the hive prepare for cold weather. All summer long they have gathered food. Now they make sure the hive is tight enough to keep out the wind. They seal up cracks with the sticky gum called propolis.

Propolis comes from thick juices on buds and some plants and trees. Bees tear the bits of gum loose with their jaws. Then they take the sticky stuff out of their mouths with their middle pair of legs and put it in the pollen baskets on their hind legs. They keep on doing this until they have large drops of glue on each pollen basket.

Back in the hive, a house bee tears the glue off the baskets by pulling at it with her jaws. It takes a lot of pulling to get the glue off, and both the house bee and the field bee hold on tight to anything rough they can find. Even then, the field bee is often pulled around as the glue is being taken off.

Bees never store propolis. As soon as the house bees get it off the field bees, they carry it in their mouths and stick it in some place that seems to need sealing up. They often drop lumps of it, and they never pick it up. The inside of a hive can get very sticky from the glue, and it can be a real nuisance to a beekeeper.

At the first signs of cold weather, the workers also make sure there are no useless bees to feed. They push all grown-up drones out of the hive. They take drone larvas from the cells and leave them outside to die, too.

Healthy worker bees and the queen will live through the winter, if they have enough food.

Turning the drones out to die

COLD WEATHER

When the temperature begins to go down, the bees form a tight cluster on the honeycomb near the wax cells where honey is stored. When it gets so chilly that you would wear a sweater outdoors, the bees turn on their own heating system. They make heat by tugging at each other, moving their bodies back and forth and fanning their wings. Scientists have found that when bees do this the temperature in the center of the cluster may rise as high as on a very hot summer day. The bees in the center work their way to the outside to cool off, and bees on the outside work their way in to the center to warm up.

The bees in the cluster eat out of the honey cells whenever they need to, but they never overeat. They have no special way of taking turns when they eat.

Bee smoker

FARMER HENRY'S BEES

Farmer Henry is a beekeeper. He takes care of many beehives. This is how he does it. When he goes close to the hives he wears a bee-veil to protect his head and face and neck from stings. The veil is attached to his hat and hangs down all around. A drawstring at the bottom pulls it close around his neck. He often wears long gloves and puts bicycle clips around his trousers. He doesn't want any bees to get inside by accident. The pressure of the clothes on the bees would make them sting.

When he goes to look inside a hive, he takes a machine called a smoker with him, and also a soft bee brush and a knife made for opening hives. The smoker is a kind of can with a bellows in it. The can is filled with leaves and other things which burn slowly. Farmer Henry lights the stuff in the can and then pumps the smoke out with the bellows.

Hive knife

Using the smoker

Before opening a hive, he squirts some smoke through the nozzle of the smoker into the entrance to the hive. Then, just as he takes the top off, he pumps in more smoke at the top. The smoke quiets the bees and makes them less likely to sting.

When Farmer Henry opens a hive he uses his special hive knife. The knife loosens the top of the hive which the bees have stuck tight with their glue. He also uses the knife to loosen the frames which hold the foundations and the honeycombs built in them.

When he lifts a frame out of the hive, he usually finds a lot of bees on it. If he wants to he can use his brush gently to wipe them off.

From time to time Farmer Henry opens the hives to see if everything is all right. If he hears the bees making a kind of whining sound, as though they were crying, he knows the queen has died, and he must get another queen for the hive. He may add a queen from another hive if he can see that a new one is about to hatch out of a big cell.

Or he may buy a queen from another beekeeper, who sends her in a tiny box or cage which has candy in it for the queen to eat. The candy is really the door to her cage. When Farmer Henry puts the cage into the hive, the bees eat through the candy door and let the queen out.

QUEEN BEE ! DELIVER QUICKL

TO

P. O.

Co.
See over

State

Mailing box
and label

When he opens the hive Farmer Henry looks to make sure the bees are storing enough bee bread for the baby bees and enough honey for themselves and for him, too. He adds more supers to the hive if they are needed.

Sometimes he finds that a sickness called "foul brood" has been killing the larvas. When he discovers this, he has to burn up the hive and the bees in it, to keep the sickness from spreading into other hives.

CATCHING SWARMS

When Farmer Henry sees bees swarming he follows them. Then he may wait until night, if that seems the best time to work with a swarm. If the swarm clusters on a limb, he cuts the limb off from the tree and then gently shakes the bees off, right in front of an empty hive he has ready. If they cluster on something that can't be cut off, he uses a bee brush and sweeps them into a big basket, or else he shakes them into it. Bees are usually good-natured when they swarm, as if they were at a party with a lot of good food inside them. They pay little or no attention to Farmer Henry, even when he walks about in the midst of the circling swarm.

Some beekeepers have even been known to get a swarm to settle on their faces, so that they look as if they had a great long beard.

Farmer Henry can take his basket full of swarming bees and pour them out in front of the new home he wants them to have. Usually they start walking toward their new hive. If they don't, Farmer Henry gently pushes them in that direction. As soon as the queen enters the hive, Farmer Henry is quite sure that they will stay in their new home.

Sometimes Farmer Henry adds a swarm to a colony that has lost its queen. He places the hive containing the swarm with the queen on the top story of the queenless colony's hive, and puts only a sheet of newspaper between them. By the time the bees have eaten through the newspaper and removed it from the hive, the colony bees and the swarm bees are used to one another and will not fight. If they were put together at once, the colony bees would attack the swarm bees as enemies, and hundreds might be killed in the battle that would follow.

At other times. Farmer Henry adds a swarm to a colony that is small. First he finds out which queen is the better, the one in the swarm or the one in the colony. He watches the two queens and chooses the one which looks healthier and lays more eggs. He kills the other, because if he put the two queens together they would fight and both might be killed. Then Farmer Henry puts the swarm with the colony in just the same way that he added a swarm to a queenless colony.

BUMBLEBEE

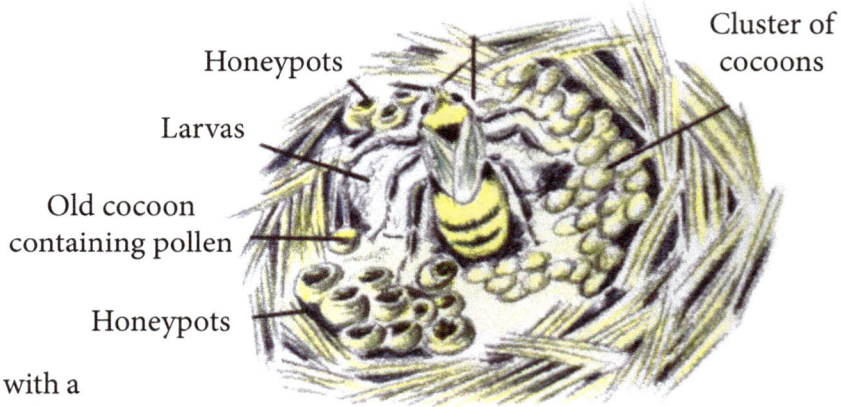

Bumblebees live in colonies, each with a queen, drones and workers. Bumblebee drones and workers do not live through the winter. Only the queen survives, spending the cold months in a hollow tree. In the spring, she finds a nest in a deserted animal's hole, or she makes a hole in the ground. She gathers nectar and pollen, storing it in a paste-like mass. After enough food has been collected, she lays eggs on the paste. When the larvas hatch, they eat the food the queen has stored. She keeps on gathering food and laying eggs until the first worker bees develop. Then they enlarge the burrow, collect food and build cells. The queen becomes only an egg-layer. The nest grows to a large community in a hole lined with straw or bits of dry plants.

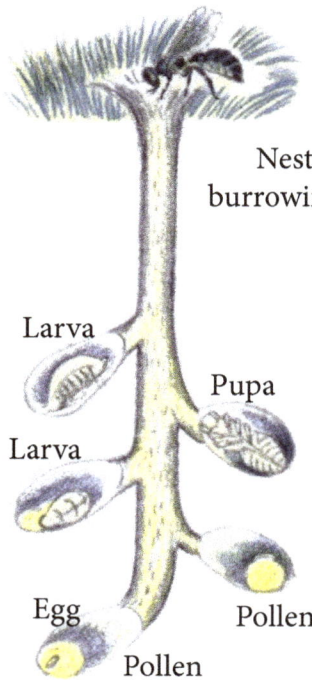

Nest of bumblebee

Honeypots

Larvas

Old cocoon containing pollen

Honeypots

Cluster of cocoons

Nest of burrowing bee

Larva

Larva

Pupa

Egg

Pollen

Pollen

BURROWING BEE

Each female burrowing bee builds her own burrow and cells, which she stocks with nectar and pollen. Two broods are hatched each year. The bees winter in the burrows and come out in the spring.

62

CARPENTER BEE

Nest of
carpenter
bee

Egg

Larva

Pupa

New bee

Carpenter bees nest in the hollowed stems of plants, which they divide into cells with plant fiber. An egg is laid in each cell. The bottom bee is first to come out, and eats its way to the cell above. The bee from each cell emerges in turn and joins the others as they crawl upward. They all wait for the top bee and leave the nest together.

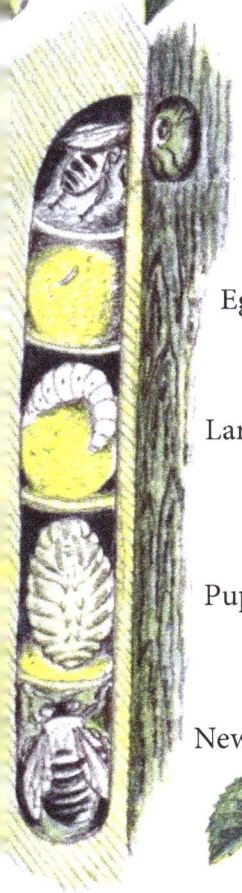

Nest of
leaf-cutting
bee

LEAF-CUTTING BEE

Leaf-cutting bees burrow in wood, hollow stems, or in the ground. With their sharp mouth parts they cut the leaves of roses and other plants into ovals and circles. The ovals are used as lining for the nests, the circles as partitions. Cells are built end to end, and stored with nectar and pollen. One egg is laid in each cell.

SHARING THE HONEY

When Farmer Henry looks into his hives and finds the top stories filled with well-cured honey, he gets ready to take his share. First he lifts up the top stories and puts a special kind of board between them and the secondstory food chamber. In the board is a little door called "a bee escape." It is built so that bees can get out through it, but cannot come back in again. In a day, most of the bees are out of the upper stories of the hive, and Farmer Henry is ready to harvest his season's honey.

He lifts out the frames which are filled with honeycomb. Then he cuts the wax tops off the cells with a special knife and puts the comb in

Farmer Henry cuts the wax
with a special knife.

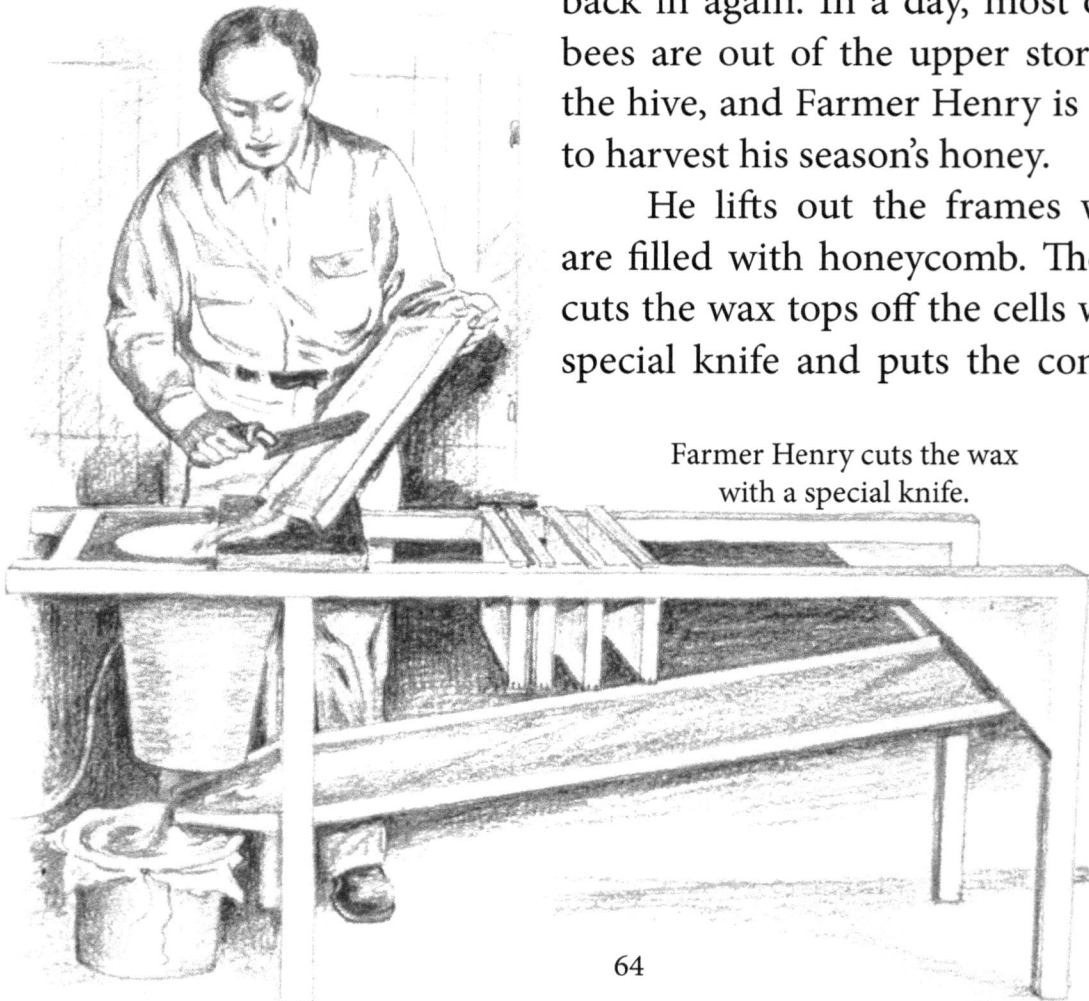

Bee escape board, in place

Bee escape board

Bee escape

a machine which whirls so fast that the honey comes out of the comb. Now he is ready to strain the honey and put it into jars, which you can buy. He is also ready to melt the wax covering he has cut off the honeycomb.

If the comb made from foundations has not broken, he can put it in frames back into the hives for the bees to use again. The broken honeycomb is melted along with the wax coverings. Farmer Henry sells this wax for making new foundations and for other uses.

When he takes his honey from the hive, Farmer Henry always leaves that which is in the two lowest stories so that the bees will have plenty of food.

Taking honey from the extractor

Honey extractor

TUCKED IN FOR THE WINTER

Farmer Henry knows that bees have their own heating system in winter, but he makes it as easy as possible for them to stay warm. He knows that guards leave the entrance in cold weather and cluster with the others on the honeycomb. This means that mice can sneak in to steal honey. So he closes up most of the entrance to keep out mice as well as the cold wind. Then he wraps the hive in a blanket of tar paper or some other material. This will help the bees keep warm even though their hive stays outdoors all winter.

MANY KINDS OF HONEY

The light-brown honey Farmer Henry collects from his bees comes mostly from apple blossoms in his orchard and from sweet clover in his neighbors' fields. But there are many other kinds of honey, and each one has its own special taste. Often you will see labels on honey jars telling what kind of flowers the honey comes

from. It may be alfalfa honey or honey from orange blossoms. Or it may be dark-colored, strong-tasting honey from buckwheat or poplar or heather blossoms. But not much dark honey is sold to use at home. Dark honey is the kind that bakers and candy-makers use to make cake and candy chewy and delicious. The honey also helps to keep these good things from drying out.

Orange blossom

Buckwheat

BEES AND PLANTS HELP EACH OTHER

Farmer Henry wouldn't have so much honey if he didn't have an orchard, but he also wouldn't have any apples unless he or someone nearby had bees. Apple trees and bees help each other, and the same thing is true of bees and orange trees and lots of other trees and flowers. This is why:

The part of a flower which grows into fruit and seeds can't develop unless it gets pollen on it. Sometimes the pollen grows in another part of the same flower. Sometimes it grows in separate flowers. When a bee crawls into a flower, some of the powdery pollen brushes off onto the fine fuzz that covers her body. She carries this pollen with her wherever she goes. And of course some tiny bits of pollen brush off again as she rubs against the flowers she visits. Some of it brushes off onto the flower part that needs pollen to help it grow into fruit.

Fruit-growers who do not raise bees often rent colonies of them from beekeepers. Some beekeepers load big trucks with their hives and move from place to place, stopping to let the bees work in orchards or in fields of clover or other plants that have a lot of nectar. In this way they get more honey than they would if they stayed in one place.

So bees help to make many of your foods besides honey. And you can see why people sometimes say, "You are as busy as a bee."

INDEX

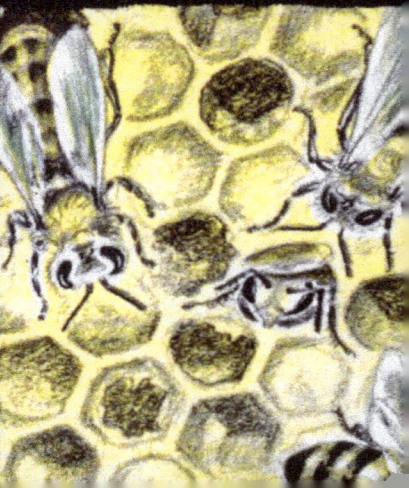